West Quayside and the Close

by

Jack and John Leslie

Published by
Newcastle Libraries & Information Service

Frontispiece:

The Close, 1973.

Acknowledgments:

Thanks to Anna Flowers, Tyne Bridge Publishing at Newcastle Libraries & Information Service, for editing this booklet, and Dilys Harding and the City Library Local Studies Section for their help and advice. Many thanks also to Ian Ayris and Frank Manders for their invaluable advice.

Photographic acknowledgements:

All photographs are copyright of Newcastle Libraries & Information Service except for nos. 3, 14, 18b: J. Marshall; nos. 4, 6, 13: City Repro; no. 15: Malcolm Maybury.

ISBN: 1 85795 1018

©Jack and John Leslie, 2001

City of Newcastle upon Tyne, Education & Libraries Directorate, Newcastle Libraries & Information Service, 2001

Front cover: The Close, 1898. Sheep being driven to the quayside.

A brief selection of further reading:

Ayris, Ian & Sheldon, Patricia, *On the Waterfront: An Historical Tour of Newcastle's Quayside*, Newcastle City Libraries & Arts, 1995.

Barke, M. & Buswell, R.J., *Newcastle's Changing Map*, Newcastle City Libraries & Arts, 1992.

Ed. Grundy, John et al, *The Buildings of England: Northumberland*, Penguin, 1992.

Pearson, Lynn, *Northern City: An Architectural History of Newcastle upon Tyne*, Newcastle City Libraries, 1996.

For your information …

Copies of photographs which are copyright of Newcastle Libraries & Information Service may be ordered and purchased from the Local Studies Section, Newcastle City Library.

City Tours visit the City and suburbs during the Summer months. A free brochure is available from Newcastle Tourist Information Service (tel: 0191 2778000).

A free brochure detailing other local history publications is also available from Newcastle City Library.

For information on any of the above contact

Tyne Bridge Publishing
City Library
Princess Square
Newcastle upon Tyne
NE99 1DX

or telephone 0191 2774174.

Visit our website at:
www.newcastle.gov.uk/tynebridgepublishing
for all the latest information.

Bygone West Quayside & the Close looks back at the history of the area bounded to the west by Forth Banks, the north by Forth Street, the east by the Side, and the south by Sandhill and the Close.

The history of Newcastle depends upon its riverside location. It was here that the Roman settlement of Pons Aelius was established, at the narrow bridging point where the banks of the Tyne rise steeply on each side. The town was concentrated here from early times, and over the centuries became very overcrowded. Land was reclaimed from the river between the thirteenth and fifteenth centuries by the tipping of rubbish behind successive waterfronts. Where the land climbs sharply to the north, the area is characterised by flights of steep stone stairs leading from the riverside to the higher ground surrounding the Castle and cathedral. On the quayside east of Sandhill the dominant feature was the narrow 'chares' or lanes stretching back at right angles to the river (largely destroyed in the fire of 1854).

With its abundance of restaurants and bars, the Sandhill area is now the focus for much of the city's thriving nightlife. In the past, however, it was a bustling commercial centre, and also the place where justice was dispensed. There is much evidence here too of the town's defensive past – the Castle Keep and the town walls.

The 'New Castle' was built in 1080, originally a wooden motte and bailey fort. It was replaced by a stone structure in the 12th and 13th centuries. During the reign of King John (1199-1216) Newcastle was in dire need of further protection from the frequent assaults by the Scots who were, according to William Gray writing in 1649, 'continually infesting and forraigning this country and rich monasteries in these Northern parts'. The incursions of the Scots prompted the building of Newcastle's defensive wall. The walls, begun in the late 13th century, were built piecemeal, during the reigns of several kings, rather than as part of a continuous plan. Remnants of the north wall can be seen in St Andrew's churchyard. The west wall still survives in long stretches running down to the Close on the edge of the River Tyne. The east wall ran from the north down to Sandgate, again on the riverside, and was built in the reign of Edward I (1272-1307). A short section of wall was also built along the river joining Sandgate to Sandhill. There was no attempt to close the gap in the wall along the river to the Close Gate in the west, probably because the town was protected by the river.

The total length of the wall was roughly two miles. Ultimately there were seven main gates providing access to and from the inner town. In addition there were also small gates known as postern gates which were created by the religious orders for their own use.

William Gray in *Chorographia* (1649) remarks that: 'in the west along the Close was Close Gate which goeth up the water [Skinner Burn] to a place of recreation called the Forth'. Most of the walls have been demolished long ago and this makes it difficult to imagine the layout and size of the town's defences.

During the 13th and 14th centuries, there were several religious orders occupying the area in and around Hanover Square and Clavering Place. Further chapels were built during later centuries. One order, the

Friars of the Sack, were so called because of the shape and material of their habits (a rough material). The Carmelites, who absorbed the friary of the Friars of the Sack in 1307, also known as the White Friars because of their white robes, took their name from their first habitation, Mount Carmel in Syria.

The medieval thoroughfare known as the Close (meaning a narrow street), which runs parallel to the river, was bounded at the east by Sandhill and in the west by Close Gate, a 14th century gate forming part of the lower portion of the walls of Newcastle. The area to the west of Close Gate was known as 'Close Without' until the gate was demolished. The street was probably developed in the 13th century on reclaimed land. The once narrow Close was widened in the mid-19th century.

Newcastle's trading prosperity was built on coal, which was transported down the Tyne and out to the ports of the South of England and beyond. The wealth created by coal meant that a healthy import and export trade of many goods grew up along the river. The flat area of land between the Close and the riverbank made it possible to construct long narrow buildings with wharves for the loading and unloading of goods. One surviving medieval merchant's house of this type may be seen at no. 35, now a restaurant. The most splendid of the buildings along the south side of the Close was the Mansion House, built 1691-2 in which Newcastle's mayor lived and where visiting dignitaries were entertained.

Up to the early 18th century the Close was mainly residential. Some prosperous and influential inhabitants included Sir John Marley (1590-1673) mayor of Newcastle, Sir William Blackett (died 1680) mayor and member of parliament for Newcastle, Sir Mark Milbank and the Earl of Northumberland.

Also in the Close were warehouses owned by wealthy merchants such as William Jenison who was mayor in 1581, and member of parliament in 1584. However, as early as 1736 Henry Bourne stated in his *History of Newcastle*: 'Of late years these Houses have been forsaken and their wealthier Inhabitants have chosen the higher Parts of the Town.' The Close and Sandhill were no longer fashionable places to live.

By the 1830s, around 60 properties stood between the old Tyne Bridge and the Forth Banks. One significant industrial building of the mid-19th century was the Phoenix Flour Mill.

The coming of the railway and the completion of the High Level Bridge in 1849 moved the commercial centre of Newcastle from the medieval core around the Close to the 'top of the hill', though the steep stairs from the Close up to the Castle Garth area were used sufficiently to support a variety of shops well into the 20th century (the High Level Bridge was a toll bridge so pedestrians tended to favour the old crossing). The area also lost its administrative presence when in January 1836 the town council decided by 25 votes to 21 that the Mansion House should cease to be the mayoral residence. Local government as well as the commercial centre thus moved away from the riverside.

The Close fell into decline for many years, but redevelopment in the later part of the 20th century has brought about something of a renaissance in this historic area of the city.

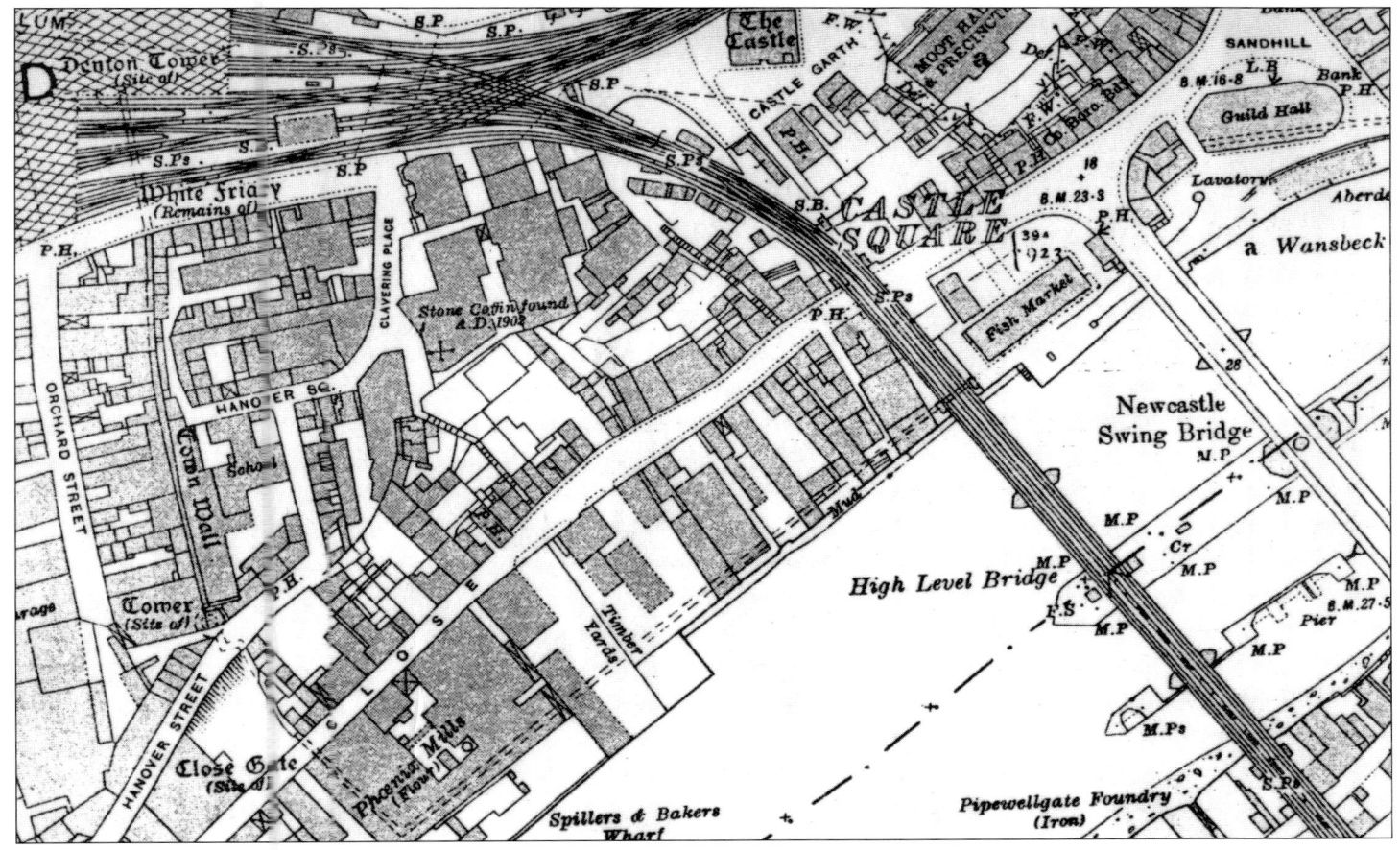

1. The Close and the west quayside area from the 1919 Ordnance Survey map of Newcastle upon Tyne, scale 25 inches to the mile. The Mansion House has been burned down but its site can be seen opposite Tuthill Stairs (leading down from Clavering Place). Long Stairs are to the left of the High Level Bridge and Castle Stairs are just opposite the Swing Bridge. The Close was widened in the mid-19th century.

2. The old Tyne Bridge of c.1250 to 1771, pictured here after the catastrophic floods of that year washed much of it away. Throughout the history of Newcastle the River Tyne has been the key factor in its commercial development. Gray's *Chorographia* (1649) describes the bridge over the Tyne as having high and broad arches and having many shops and houses on it. There were three towers, one at each end and one in the middle. The tower at the Newcastle end was used as a chapel: St. Thomas the Martyr. The bridge also accommodated a prison. By 1781 a stone bridge had replaced the medieval bridge, but it was always too narrow, and its low arches stopped larger river traffic from getting upriver. In 1876 the Swing Bridge was opened.

3. The High Level Bridge. One of the massive arch supports of this road and rail bridge stands in the Close. On 29 August 1848 the first railway crossing of the River Tyne from Gateshead to Newcastle was undertaken across a line of rails constructed on scaffolding on the new bridge. The mayor and guests travelled across this temporary structure in eight carriages pulled by a highly decorated engine. The erection of the High Level Bridge and viaducts necessitated the removal of 655 families in Newcastle and 130 in Gateshead. The splendid bridge was not officially opened until 1849 and the road deck was opened in February 1850. On 28 July 1849 John Smith, a carpenter working on the rail deck of the bridge, stepped on a loose plank and toppled headfirst over the edge. During his fall, the leg of his fustian trousers caught on a large nail which had been driven into the timber above the level of the road deck, some 90 feet above the river. Here he was suspended until rescued by workmen. The picture shows the bridge in 1955 with the Close beyond.

4. The Swing Bridge. In 1876 the stone bridge which had replaced the medieval Tyne Bridge was itself replaced by W.G. Armstrong's Swing Bridge which opened onto Sandhill. The hydraulic mechanism which opens and closes the bridge allowed Sir William and his company to build ships at Elswick and sail them down the Tyne to destinations all over the world. This photograph shows the Swing Bridge in 1966 looking from Gateshead over to Sandhill and the Close. Since the Romans built Pons Aelius there has always been a bridge on the site of the Swing Bridge. Beyond the Swing Bridge looms the Moot Hall (built as the County Court and prison near the site of the original moot hall in 1810-1).

5. Sandhill in 1884, originally literally a hill of sand. From the 14th century it was a market and recreation ground, and later accommodated a bullring, closed by magistrates in 1768 after a fatal goring. Most of the restored buildings, including the splendidly timbered Bessie Surtees House (centre), and Milbank House to its left (the earliest parts dating from the 14th century), are there today and an inkling of the former opulence of the housing in the Close and on Sandhill can be gathered. The houses were renovated in the 1930s. The Guildhall is to the left, originally part of the Exchange and Town Hall. Rebuilt in the 1650s it has been altered over the years. In 1823 a colonnaded fish market was designed by John Dobson and added to the east end of the Guildhall. Until the late 17th century a tidal stream, the Lort Burn, bisected the east side of Sandhill.

6. The Wholesale Fish Market was the subject of much controversy in 1878 when there were objections to its being built on the river's edge. The building was intended to replace John Dobson's colonnaded extension to the Guildhall of 1823. Finally erected in 1880, the fish market traded there until 1916 when business transferred to the Clayton Street fish market. Neptune House, as it is now known, was designed by A.M. Fowler and retains many of its original features including statues of Neptune and fishwives atop the quayside entrance. It stands on land which was once occupied by the Earl of Northumberland's houses between the narrow alley known as Javel Groupe and the old Tyne Bridge. The name Javel Groupe is derived from 'gavell' referring to the gaol in the Castle Keep above, and 'group' meaning a stream or channel.

This photograph was taken in 1982. The steep bank of the Tyne rising above the Close is well illustrated. Just visible behind the Keep and the railway viaduct are the Black Gate and Castle Garth. The rear of the Bridge Hotel is tucked to the right of the High Level Bridge. Castle Stairs are just to the right of the Fish Market.

7. The Close, 1898. From medieval times until the middle of the 17th century the Close was mainly residential and inhabited by the prosperous and influential. There were around 60 properties between the old Tyne Bridge and Forth Banks. Before the demolition of Close Gate, which was situated where the town wall crossed the lane, the Close was divided into the Close Within and the Close Without (inside or outside the gate). Later it was simply the Close. In this photograph sheep are being driven down to the quayside. A tragic story involving a sheep tells that in 1758 two dyers, named Clowney and Porteous, washing cloth on 'stands', in the river were knocked into the water and drowned when a sheep escaping from a nearby butchers was chased by a dog and leaped from the quay.

8. Arthur's Cooperage, c.1879. In 1553 an Act of Parliament stated that there should be no more than four taverns or ale houses in the whole of Newcastle. In 1855 however, according to Wards Directory, there were no less then eleven drinking establishments in the Close alone! These hostelries included the Beehive, the Duke of Cumberland, the Cannon, the Blue Jug, the Tiger, the Dolphin, and the Wagon.

The earliest part of the timber-framed Cooperage at no. 32 the Close dates from the 15th century. It started out as the home and business premises of one of the wealthy merchants who lived in this area of the town. John Arthur, a cooper (barrel maker), had his premises nearby according to records of 1730. In 1863 the business moved into this building which took on the name of the trade it has since been associated with. It was not until 1973 that it was converted into a pub and restaurant. It is reputed to be one of the most haunted buildings in Newcastle. The stairs just to the right are Long Stairs.

9. The foundation stone of the old Mansion House, opposite the foot of Tuthill Stairs, was laid in 1691 and the cost of the brick turreted building was £6,000. The mayor resided here during his term of office and would entertain visiting judges who were presiding at the Assizes. However, the lower part of the town was being deserted by the wealthy by the late 18th century and was described as 'extremely ineligible, being almost continually enveloped in smoke and soot'. In 1836 the Town Council decided the Mansion House should cease to be the state house of the corporation but it was not until 1865 that no. 1 Ellison Place was acquired for this purpose. The contents of the old Mansion House (including 23 feather beds) were sold off. The former Mansion House then became a timber warehouse, surviving until 1895 when it was destroyed by fire. The site is now occupied by the modern office block of Bridge House. The photograph shows the remains of the Mansion House from Tuthill Stairs in 1885, and inset is a view of it in better days, c.1827.

10. A medieval doorway in the Close, 1886. The Close was originally bounded to the west by the 14th century Close Gate, which formed part of the lower portion of the town walls. Close Gate was damaged during the Civil War siege of 1644 when the walls were breached. It was repaired in 1648 and used as a temporary prison after the floods of 17th November 1771 swept away four of the arches of the Tyne Bridge and the prison which stood upon it. The gate had previously functioned as a meeting house for the guild of the House Carpenters Company. It was finally demolished on 22nd November 1797 'on account of obstructing traffic in that street, as waggons frequently stuck fast in the narrow gateway'. The site of the gate is marked by a plaque on the north side of the Close. The stretch of wall from Close Gate to the river, and part of the riverside tower and shore wall, was revealed by an excavation when the Copthorne Hotel was being developed. The piling of the hotel straddles the line of the wall.

11. Clavering Place, 1882. Situated on the high ground above the Close, and reached directly from the Close by Tuthill Stairs, this was one of several middle-class residential developments built inside the town walls during the 18th century. Others included Hanover Square and Charlotte Square (off Westgate Road). The elegant Clavering House, built around 1784, a brick building, is a reminder that before the railway viaduct was completed in 1849 this was a fashionable residential area of the 1780s, with several large houses. Opposite Clavering House is a Presbyterian chapel of 1822.

12. Hanover Square dates back to 1720. The Square, with its associations with the Carmelite order of White Friars contained a number of chapels. Hanover Square Chapel became a tobacco and snuff factory and today is partially occupied by a local business. Hanover Square also contained a charity school, a brewery which dated back to 1790 and eventually became Northern Clubs Federation Brewery, St James's Mission Hall, and dwellings. This photograph shows the entrance to Hanover Square from Clavering Place in 1886.

13. Hanover Street runs from Hanover Square down to the Close. On the north side stood the White Friars' Tower, part of the Town Wall, which later became a meeting house for the guild of Bricklayers and Meters (measurers of corn etc). When the tower was pulled down in 1840, Roman remains were discovered beneath, including an altar (transferred to the Keep). The bonded warehouses with their giant numbers, built 1841-4, on the right of this 1989 photograph have mostly been demolished following a series of fires during the 1990s. The Shap granite cast-way running up the centre of the street provided a smoother ride and better grip for vehicles going up the steep hill.

14. Hanover Stairs, 1985. The very steep banks of the Tyne below the Castle Keep necessitated the construction of steep stairs down to the riverside. Hanover Stairs ran down from Hanover Street through the middle of the bonded warehouse buildings to emerge at the bottom on to the Close. This configuration makes the stairs quite unique. The stairs were built to facilitate access to Hanover Street for the benefit of the warehouses, but their value as a short cut was not lost on the general public who found they could descend from Hanover Street under the cover of the stairs. The tall thin entry to the stairs lies between warehouses built for, and probably by, Amos Spoor in 1841-1844. The stately warehouses are now very damaged and Hanover Stairs are closed off.

15. Breakneck Stairs actually formed part of the western town wall leading up from Close Gate to the top of the White Friars stretch of the wall. The total length of the stairs was some 60 yards and there were 140 steps covering this distance. As their name implies, Breakneck Stairs were very hazardous, being extremely steep. Today this part of the wall from the Close to Hanover Street can still be seen and some of Breakneck Stairs are clearly visible though not accessible. This photograph, taken in 1998, shows the remains of the stairs built into the town wall (bottom left). The Copthorne Hotel stands directly opposite, and the floor of the hotel incorporates brass plates showing the line of the wall.

16. Tuthill Stairs are approximately 140 yards east of Breakneck Stairs. Over the years there have been many different spellings of the name of this set of stairs, for example 'Tooterhil', 'Tudhill', 'Touthill' and 'Towtehill'. These stairs lead from the Close, opposite the site of the Mansion House, up to Hanover Square and Clavering Place. It is generally accepted the 'tout' of the name derived from the lookout who could see any threat from the Gateshead bank to the only part of the town that was not walled. However Henry Bourne in 1732 gives this description; 'I have been somewhere informed of, that the proper name of it should be Tout-hill, from the touting or winding of a horn upon it, when an Enemy was at hand.'

Records show that in 1859 a chapel stood on Tuthill Stairs, and also a number of businesses and residences. These included T. Hunter a slater, J. Chambers and J. Dixon both grocers. The chapel which was occupied by the Baptists from 1797 to around 1853 was ultimately converted into tenements. The picture shows a very dilapidated Tuthill Stairs in 1879. The posters are advertising excursions to Ripon and Leeds, and one to Rothbury costing three shillings. The Tyne Regatta is also heralded.

17. Castle Garth. At the top of Castle Stairs stands the Castle Keep, and the area around it, the Castle Garth or yard. This area and nearby Castle Square were very busy commercially in the early 19th century when the Square boasted two inns (the Castle and the New Bridge, now rebuilt as the Bridge Hotel), two chimney sweeps, a grocer, two clothes dealers and a dealer in 'sundry items'. In the Garth were four tailors, three bootmakers, four clothes dealers, a painter, a hatter and a bricklayers' hall. An interesting notice which appeared in 1792 illustrates the diversity of activities on and around the stairs:

> *To be let, the Old Castle in the Castle Garth, upon which, with the greatest convenience and advantage may be erected a Wind-Mill for the purpose of grinding Corn and Bolting flour, or making Oil etc. There is exceeding good spring of water within the Castle. which renders it a very eligible situation for a Brewery, or any manufactory that requires a constant supply of water. The proprietor, upon proper terms, will be at considerable part of the expense. Enquire Mr Fryer, in Westgate Street Newcastle. September 14th 1782.*

The photograph shows Castle Garth in 1883. The entrance to Dog Leap Stairs is shown at the far right. The narrow alley opposite the Moot Hall has long been cleared of the old buildings.

18. Dog Leap Stairs were important as an access to the east postern (gateway) of the Castle from the Side. 'Dog Leap', or 'Dog Loup' as they were sometimes known, refers to a narrow slip of ground between houses. A popular story relates to John Scott, later Lord Eldon and Lord Chancellor, and his elopement with the heiress Bessie Surtees in 1772. It is said that John and his intended bride, after her descent by ladder from the Surtees house on Sandhill, escaped on horseback up Dog Leap Stairs, which must have been very hard indeed on the horse! The main photograph shows Castle Garth and the top of Dog Leap Stairs in the 1890s. The rear of the Black Gate looms at the end of the alley.
Inset: looking down Dog Leap Stairs to the Side in 1950.

19. Castle Stairs, built of tough Scottish granite, lead from the Close up to Castle Garth. In 1828 clothes dealers were the most numerous of the businesses located on the stairs. There were ten of them. A little later in 1855 things had changed and the stairs must have been a hive of industry with sixteen firms of boot makers operating from their confines. Also operating from Castle Stairs at this time were J. Henderson & Son cabinet makers, D. Laird and T. Thornton, both clothes dealers, and C. Waters, a rope manufacturer. Just over a hundred years later in 1968 there was only Jas. Jobling the hairdresser operating from Castle Stairs. Today we can see a restored medieval well to the right of the first landing. The remains of small gardens to be seen to the left and right of Castle Stairs are all that is left of the 'burgage plots' which once belonged to the tall merchants' houses which fronted on to the Close.

This photograph, looking down to the Close, shows boot making businesses, including 'T, Bartlett', operating from the stairs in 1924. The low entry is now opened up.

20. Long Stairs, to the east of Tuthill Stairs, lead from the Close to Queen Street, now Queens Lane, and the entrance to the High Level Bridge. At the head of the stairs there is a path to Castle Stairs and the Castle. In 1801 the links between Long Stairs and Castle Stairs comprised Bankside and an arched passage quaintly called Sheep-Head Alley. As opposed to other stairs which housed many businesses, in 1859 a solitary chimney sweep, J. Hindmarch, had his premises on Long Stairs. This photograph shows the stairs in derelict condition in 1962.